Th[illegible] Holy Spirit & You

LoveWorld Publications

THE HOLY SPIRIT AND YOU

ISBN 978-37061-5-2

All scripture quotations are taken from the King James Version of the Bible unless otherwise indicated.

UNITED KINGDOM:
Christ Embassy Int'l Office
363 Springfield Road
Chelmsford
Essex, CM2 6AW
Tel:+44 1245 490 234

USA:
Christ Embassy USA,
7425 Forbes BLVD
Suite 205 Lanham,
MD 20706
Tel:+1-301-860 0703

SOUTH AFRICA:
303 Pretoria Avenue
Cnr. Harley and Hendrik Vewoerd,
Randburg, Gauteng
South Africa.
Tel: +27-72-241 7332

CANADA:
2304, Sheppard Avenue
West Toronto M9M 1M1
Tel/Fax:+1-416-746 5080

NIGERIA:
P.O. Box 13563
Ikeja, Lagos.
Tel:+234-802 3324 188,
+234-805 2464 131,
+234-1-892 5724

email: cec@christembassy.org
website: www.christembassy.org

Contents

Introduction

When a man is not born again, he's ignorant of the things he doesn't know. He's so blind that he can't tell what he doesn't know because he walks according to his senses. If you're born again, you're different from the world. Your eyes have been rubbed with the eye-salve of the Spirit of God, and now you can see! The Bible says,

> ***"Now we have received, not the spirit of the world, but the spirit which is of God; that we might know** (comprehend, grasp) **the things that are freely given to us of God. Which things also we speak, not in the words which man's wisdom teacheth, but which the Holy Ghost teacheth; comparing spiritual things with spiritual. But the natural man receiveth not the things of the Spirit of God: for they are foolishness unto him: neither can he know them, because they are spiritually discerned"***
>
> **(1 Corinthians 2:12-14).**

Paul, while writing this scripture, wasn't referring to mental knowledge but revelation knowledge – specific, exact and absolute knowledge. It is possible for us to **know** the will of God for our lives. The Bible says it can only be spiritually understood; it can only be grasped by the spirit of man. When your human spirit is enlightened by God's Word, then you are able to ***know*** God's will for you.

God's Word is the Light that shines on your path (Psalm 119:105). However, the fact that the light is shining on your path doesn't mean you're traveling the exact route you should, for there could be several routes along your path. This is where the guidance of the Holy Spirit comes in. He's the One Who guides your steps into the right route along your path. He also opens your understanding of the Word, and teaches you what is right from the Scriptures.

You may be at a crossroads in your life right now and asking, "Where do I go from here?" You need a Guide to lead you; that Guide is the Holy Spirit. Knowing Him and walking with Him is the key to that successful life you've always desired. He brings you into your inheritance and your destiny in God.

Chapter One

Get to Know the Holy Spirit

The Holy Spirit of God is not some smoke or cloud, nor is He a light. He is not a thing! The Holy Spirit is the third Person of the Godhead. Why do we call Him the third Person of the Godhead when, in fact, He's the first Person to be revealed in the

Scriptures? This is because He's the last of the Trinity to be known by us. When you study in Genesis chapter one, it says, "In the beginning God (Elohim) created the heaven and the earth" (Genesis 1:1).

'Elohim' in Hebrew, is plural for 'God.' We are then told that the Spirit of God moved over the face of the deep. Thus, even though the Holy Spirit is the first to be revealed from 'Elohim,' He is the last that we get acquainted with, because Jesus said to His disciples in **John 14:15-17,**

> ***"If ye love me, keep my commandments. And I will pray the Father, and he shall give you another Comforter, that he may abide with you for ever; Even the Spirit of truth; whom the world cannot receive, because it seeth him not,***

> ***neither knoweth him: but ye know him; for he dwelleth with you, and shall be in you."***

The Holy Spirit is exactly like Jesus. He does not receive power from God. In fact, He is the POWER of God! The Holy Spirit is the Spirit of truth which proceeds from the Father. He is not less than the Father, nor is He less than Jesus. He proceeds from the Father.

If you went to heaven, you wouldn't find the Holy Ghost outside the Father, for He is in the Father. On earth, you'll find Him everywhere! Why is this so? It's because everywhere you go as a child of God, the Holy Ghost goes with you and His presence rubs upon everything that concerns you.

What's His Name?

"But the Comforter, which is the Holy Ghost, whom the Father will send in my name..."

(John 14:26).

This verse simply implies that the Father will say to the Holy Ghost, "Go in the Name of Jesus..." The Holy Ghost was sent by the Father in the Name of Jesus. The Holy Ghost doesn't have a name; His name is not 'Holy Ghost' or 'Holy Spirit.' That's just a description of His person, His character. The Holy Ghost has no name of His own, but He answers to the Name of Jesus.

When you call the Name 'Jesus,' the Holy Ghost goes into action. He will have no right to function in the earth the way He does, except if He came in the Name of

Someone that had a right to the earth. Jesus bought the whole world. He's called the Son of man and the Son of God; He's 100 percent man and 100 percent God. He's the One with the right to the whole world. He's the Seed of Abraham.

Now the Holy Ghost has come to earth in the Name of Jesus. He takes the place of Jesus here on earth. He's here to do whatever Jesus would have done. He's not less powerful than Jesus. In fact, He was the One Who empowered Jesus.

The Bible says in **Acts 10:38**,

> ***"How God anointed Jesus of Nazareth with the Holy Ghost and with power: who went about doing good, and healing all that were oppressed of the devil; for God was with him."***

He was that Power. Now Jesus is gone to heaven but the Holy Ghost is here with us. He's here to help us claim everything that belongs to Jesus. We are His heirs; joint heirs with Christ. The Bible says in **1 Corinthians 2:12,**

> ***"Now we have received, not the spirit of the world, but the spirit which is of God; that we might know the things that are freely given to us of God..."***

The One with whom we're dealing owns the whole world. The Holy Ghost is not here to beg anybody. He's here in the Name of the Seed of Abraham. Remember, God Almighty willed the whole world to Abraham and to his Seed.

The Bible says that the Seed of Abraham is Christ and if you belong to Christ, you are Abraham's seed and therefore, heirs according to the promise (Galatians 3:29). That's why I just can't accept poverty. Nobody is going to hand poverty over to me. I refuse to be described as poor because I'm not. I'm Abraham's seed. I know who I am. I'm not an ordinary person; I'm an heir of God and a joint-heir with Christ! (Romans 8:17).

There's a place for you in God. It's a place of health where you have dominion over sickness and disease. It's a place of wealth where lack, want and poverty are all aliens. There's such a place and that's where I live.

Paul describes this ethereal place in Hebrews 12:22:

> ***"But ye are come unto mount Sion, and unto the city of the***

living God, the heavenly Jerusalem, and to an innumerable company of angels"

(Hebrews 12:22).

Every time I meet a brother or sister who's from this place, I know it. I've seen some of them. I also know those who are still looking for this place. They're trying to get there but it's no use, because you ought to be born in there! Many are babies in there and don't know what it is to live there. Some others have strayed out of there to some other city, but the life in the city I'm talking about is one way only.

I read a beautiful story about Smith Wigglesworth. It was said that he was out when his wife died. When he returned home and was told his wife had died, he said, "She didn't tell me before she died. How could she die without permission?"

He then laid hands on her in the Name of Jesus Christ of Nazareth and called her back to life. She woke up and he asked her why she didn't inform him she was going to die. She told him it was time for her to go and that she really wanted to go. So he said "It's alright, but you should have told me." Then he let her sleep and she was gone. That's a man from our city!

Believe this: When the Holy Spirit comes to live in you, you become His headquarters; His centre of operation. He comes alive in your body and makes it His home.

> ***"And be not drunk with wine, wherein is excess; but be filled with the Spirit;"***
>
> **(Ephesians 5:18).**

God is saying to us here that He desires that we receive the infilling of the Holy Spirit, whereby He fills us with all of His fullness. This is done so we can experience His power as He imparts our spirits with the divine enablement to live the victorious Christian life.

"How do I receive the infilling of the Holy Spirit?" you may ask.

There are several ways to receive the infilling of the Holy Spirit. During Apostle Paul's missionary journey through Asia, he met twelve men in Ephesus, who had not received the Holy Spirit.

The Bible records that *"...when Paul had laid his hands upon them, the Holy Ghost came on them; and they spake with tongues, and prophesied"* (Acts 19:6).

This is one of the ways to receive the

infilling of the Holy Spirit. Those men had to have someone else, who had received the fullness of the Spirit, lay hands upon them. If you have not received the infilling of the Holy Spirit, you can have someone (who's full of the Spirit) lay hands on you and you'll receive.

Another way to receive the Holy Spirit is by asking in prayer. The Lord said in **Luke 11:13,**

> ***"If ye then, being evil, know how to give good gifts unto your children: how much more shall your heavenly Father give the Holy Spirit to them that ask Him?"***

This means when you ask the Father in faith and in the Name of the Lord Jesus, you will receive the Holy Spirit.

You might be reading this book now and it could be that your grandparents were poor people. In fact, everybody in your family has been poor. Now, here you are on the scene and you can hear every voice telling you, "Hey, you're already poor; you can't reach for anything more. You're poor, you've always been poor and you'll always be poor!"

If you have in your life this Person I'm introducing to you, then you will hear His voice in you. He will lead you through the wilderness of life and direct your steps. He will tell you what to do and inspire the right thoughts in you. He will give you an earth-shaking idea. He will show you a vision of what He sees you to be. The Holy Spirit will set a picture before you and help you journey towards that picture!

Chapter Two

The Ministry of the Holy Spirit

After your salvation, the greatest experience you could ever have in your life is the experience with the unseen Person of the Holy Spirit. 'Holy Ghost' and 'Holy Spirit' refer to the same Person. The King James Version uses the term 'Holy Ghost' but I will be using both terms interchangeably in this book. Wherever you see the words 'Holy Ghost' and 'Holy Spirit,' understand that I'm talking about one and the same Person.

The Comforter

"And I will pray the Father, and he shall give you another Comforter, that he may abide with you for ever; Even the Spirit of truth; whom the world cannot receive, because it seeth him not, neither knoweth him: but ye know him; for he dwelleth with you, and shall be in you."

(John 14:16-17).

Jesus, talking to His disciples in one of the last meetings He had with them before He was crucified, told them He was going away to be with the Father. As He told them these things, His disciples were sad because they wondered how they would cope without Him.

Then in the sixteenth verse, He said to them, ***"...I will pray** (ask) **the Father and He shall give you another Comforter**..."* Now, that suggests that Jesus was the Comforter and He was going to ask the Father to send them another Comforter just like Him.

There are two words for *'another'* in the Greek: one is *'Heteros'* and the other is *'Allos.' Heteros* means 'another one of a different kind,' while *Allos* means 'another one of the same kind.'

Jesus chose the word 'Allos' instead of

'Heteros.' He didn't say, "I will pray the Father and He shall give you *Heteros Parakletos.*" He said, "I will pray the Father and He shall give you *Allos Parakletos,*" meaning 'another one of the same kind of *Paraklet.*' *Parakletos,* referring to One called to go alongside.

Now, the first word given to us for *Paraklet* in the English language is *'Comforter.'* In other words, a Paraklet is 'one who is called to go with you as a comforter.'

But what kind of *Comforter* was Jesus talking about? Was He talking about a passive helper, one who just says, "Oh, don't worry about the problem, every thing is going to be alright"? Was He talking about One who'll suffer with you when you suffer or tell you, "Don't worry, move forward, I'll be with you?" Was that the kind of Comforter Jesus was talking about? Absolutely not!

The Amplified Bible translation lets us know that the Comforter Who has been sent to go along with us is pro-active by giving us six synonyms of the word "Comforter" (Parakletos). They are *Counsellor, Helper, Intercessor, Advocate, Strengthener* and *Standby.*

The Counsellor

> ***"And I will ask the Father, and He will give you another Comforter (Counselor, Helper, Intercessor, Advocate, Strengthener, and Standby), that He may remain with you forever..."***

(John 14:16 Amp).

When you receive the Holy Spirit, He becomes your Counsellor. He is the One who gives you advice, but the kind of advice He gives is not passive. The word 'counsellor' is a legal term which means 'legal adviser.' This simply implies that as your Counsellor, the Holy Spirit gives you legal advice, He becomes your lawyer.

> ***"I will bless the LORD, who hath given me counsel: my reins also instruct me in the night seasons"***
>
> **(Psalm 16:7).**

The Psalmist acknowledged that it was the Lord Who gave him counsel. 'My reins' here means 'my inward man.' So this scripture could read, "I'm instructed in my inward man in the night seasons." It is the Holy Spirit Who instructs you in your inward man. He gives you instructions by which He guides your life.

There are issues of life not expressly dealt with in the Scriptures for which you require guidance. For example, things that concern daily living such as decision-making, traveling or even making purchases. Perhaps you want to see a friend and you want to know whether he's in or not. There's no way you can tell that if you search the Bible from Genesis to Revelation. But you can hear the Holy Spirit speak to you. You can walk in His counsel and make the right choices and decisions in your life.

One day, while Peter was praying in the house of Simon the tanner, the Spirit of God said to him, "Three men seek you, I sent them. Go with them."

"And, behold, immediately there were three men already come unto the house where I was, sent from Caesarea unto me. And the spirit bade me go with them..."

(Acts 11:11-12).

Peter said, "The Spirit bade me go..." The Holy Spirit can tell you to do something and He can tell you not to. He can direct you. Has He ever told you to do anything? Has He instructed you about anything before? Are you acquainted with the Counsellor or do you find yourself always getting advice from people? Let the Holy Spirit function in you. He'll talk to you and instruct you.

If you made a new friend, you'd have to spend some time with him to know him and understand his language. In the same way, you need to spend time with the Holy Spirit. You need to take time to understand His language so that you can recognize His voice when He speaks to you. Start today to follow His leading in your decisions and actions as you consistently meditate on the Word and fellowship with Him.

The Helper

The Holy Spirit is also your Helper. When you receive Him into your life, you should never say again, "I don't have anybody to help me," because He's your Helper.

While meditating many years ago, the Holy Spirit inspired this thought in me and I penned it down. I wrote, "God has the right people in the right place to help me at the right time." Why? It's because the Holy Ghost is my Helper and when He needs to use somebody to help me, He'll get anybody to do it. He's my Helper and He can assign anybody to it. There are people who will help me even when they don't want to, because the Holy Ghost compels them to.

You've got to become positive about life and I'm not just talking about positive thinking. I'm talking about being positive according to the Kingdom principles of life. And this is why you should be positive: God made the world and put you here, evidently showing that He loves you. Why then should you talk as if He doesn't want you? If He doesn't want you, He'll just get rid of you without asking you any questions. He doesn't need to obtain permission from you to do that.

The fact that God has let you live is to show you that He wants you, and if He truly does, why then will He want you to suffer? What does He get from your suffering?

The Bible says in **Acts chapter 10 verse 38**:

> ***"How God anointed Jesus of Nazareth with the Holy Ghost and with power, who went about doing good and healing all that were oppressed of the devil for God was with Him."***

God anointed Jesus and sent Him to heal those that were oppressed of the devil, which means, God wanted them to be well. Therefore, He is a good God.

The Church of Jesus Christ is not a group

of people seeking help from God. We have One called to go with us and that's His ministry. We're not alone. When you look at us and think that all you see about us is all there is, then you're wrong. There's Someone Who's not only with us but also lives in us. You may not see Him with your optical eyes but He's right there. In fact, He's more present than our adversaries.

The psalmist calls the Holy Spirit ***a very present help*** in trouble (Psalm 46:1). When he says 'a very present help,' it doesn't mean the Holy Spirit is one out of the many 'present helps.' By attaching the 'very' to the 'present help' the psalmist lets us know he's referring to a definite personality, in spite of the generic tone that the 'a' suggests.

He could simply have said, "He is *a present help* in trouble," instead he strengthens it by saying, "He's *'a **very** present'* help." In other words, His presence with you is something you don't need to doubt at all. You don't have to look for Him. If you ever get into trouble, you might as well laugh and say, "Thank You Holy Spirit, I'm not alone!"

God never gives us the impression that we're disadvantaged in any way. You ought not to be disadvantaged. If you find yourself disadvantaged, then you put yourself there. If you're in a predicament, even if you didn't put yourself in it, you're responsible for keeping yourself in it because God has given you all that you require to emerge victoriously from every situation.

The Intercessor

The Holy Spirit goes with you as your *Intercessor,* but He also carries out His intercessory ministry through you, a believer.

If a Christian has a problem or is in trouble, the Holy Spirit is the One who will pray for him. Does He do this by Himself? No, He doesn't. How could God pray for you by Himself? It would be illegal for Him to do that. He prays for us only through another believer in Christ Jesus who's filled with the Spirit. The Holy Spirit is not human. He doesn't have a human body, so He works through us.

To explain that with the scriptures, let's take a look at **Romans 8:26:**

"Likewise the Spirit also helpeth

> ***our infirmities: for we know not what we should pray for as we ought: but the Spirit itself*** *(Himself)* ***maketh intercession for us with groanings which cannot be uttered."***

A lot of other translations use the word 'weaknesses' in place of 'infirmities' but it still doesn't communicate it strongly enough. That's why I like the J.B. Philips' translation of this verse. It uses the word 'limitations' instead of 'infirmities' or 'weaknesses.'

> ***"...for we know not what we should pray for as we ought..."***

This means we don't always know what we should pray for, and how to pray about them,

> ***"...but the Spirit himself maketh intercession for us with groanings which cannot be uttered."***

Now, if you've been following this carefully, you'll understand that the Holy Spirit is not doing this apart from us but through us, because He dwells in us. That is why the Bible says, *"...the Spirit Himself makes intercession for us with groanings which cannot be uttered."* You should understand that this is different from speaking in tongues.

> ***"For if I pray in an unknown tongue, my spirit prayeth, but my understanding is unfruitful"***
>
> **(1 Corinthians 14:14).**

When you're talking in tongues, you don't know what you're saying because it's your spirit talking. But in this case, the Bible says, the Holy Ghost Himself makes intercession for us with groanings which cannot be uttered or as the *New Revised Standard Version* puts it, *'sighs too deep for words.'*

There are times when you find yourself crying or making loud groans. At such times, you're actually unable to articulate what you have inside in tongues or any other language because it is too deep for words.

The Bible says in **Romans 8:27**, ***"And he that searcheth the hearts*** (that means, He that searches the spirit of man) ***knoweth what is the mind of the Spirit."***

'He that searches the heart' is God Who knows what the mind of the Spirit is, and the Spirit knows how to make intercession for the saints according to the will of God.

The Bible goes on to say in **verse 28**,

> ***"And we know that all things work together for good to them that love God, to them who are the called according to his purpose."***

So, the Spirit of God intercedes for His people through other believers. He doesn't do it all by Himself; He needs to do it through us. He heals the sick and leads men and women to Christ through us.

A very beautiful teaching along this line is what we have in Acts chapter 10 - the story of Cornelius, the Roman centurion. God wanted to save Cornelius because he had been so kind and was looking for salvation. So He had mercy on him and sent an angel to him with this message: "Your prayers and your alms have come up for a memorial before God" (Acts 10:4).

The angel couldn't lead Cornelius to Christ because it's not the responsibility of angels to lead people to Christ. They do not have that honour. Even the Holy Ghost, all by Himself, couldn't have done beyond what He did.

All the angel could do was deliver the message: "Send men to Joppa, and call for Simon whose surname is Peter. He will tell you words by which you and all your household will be saved." Thus, Cornelius was saved by words – words that conveyed to him the plan of God for salvation. There's no other way a man can be saved.

Look at Jesus. He spoke out of heaven to Saul of Tarsus whom He called by name. He said to him, "Saul, Saul, why do you persecute Me? It's hard for you to kick against the pricks" (Acts 9:4, 5). He then told Saul to go into the city where he would be told what to do.

Guess what the Lord did? He appeared in a vision to a man named Ananias and said to him, "Go into the street called 'Straight.' There you will find a man named Saul of Tarsus." The Lord didn't need to give him more description, Ananias already knew who He was talking about.

"But Lord, that man is making havoc of the Church!" Ananias protested.

"Don't worry," the Lord replied, "he's been disciplined. I just knocked his sight out and he's blind right now. You go lay hands on him and tell him to receive his sight."

So Ananias went there and ministered to Saul. Why didn't the Lord do it all by Himself? The reason is that the ministry of reconciliation has been given to man. The Bible says He (God) *"...hath given to us the ministry of reconciliation"* (2 Corinthians 5:18). The Holy Spirit carries out His intercessory ministry through us.

It's great to know we have an intercessor who's praying for us in the background, but there's more. When Jesus told us He would send us another intercessor, He was not just looking at someone at the background. He gives us another word to strengthen the thought. He says He is our Advocate!

The Advocate

The kind of intercessor the Holy Ghost is to us is that of an advocate – a counsel for the defence. He's our legal representative. He speaks on our behalf; He defends us. So when Jesus said, *"...I will pray the Father, and he shall give you another Comforter..."* He was talking about Someone Who engages our adversaries; Someone Who comes right into the middle of the heat and takes charge with us, not someone who watches us from the background as we grapple with forces and circumstances that assail us.

You can never be disadvantaged anymore. When people are saying evil things about you and have judged you wrongly, don't worry. Your Advocate will be right there. They may not give you an opportunity for defence or explanation. Your Counsel for the defence will show up at the right time. You just keep saying this: "I can never be disadvantaged. I can never be discouraged," praise the Lord!

The Strengthener

The Holy Spirit also ministers to you as your 'Strengthener.' The reason He strengthens you is so that while He's taking His own steps to ensure that everything works out right for you, you are also participating actively in the process, since He has to function through you.

If you have the Holy Ghost in your life, weakness no longer describes you. No wonder Paul said, ***"...when I am weak then am I strong."*** In other words, when he was bruised and battered; broken down by outside factors, he was made even stronger by the power of the Holy Ghost.

Have you ever felt yourself so weak and

without strength that it seemed like everything was going dark. I hear that some people sometimes pass out because they have high blood pressure. They black out all of a sudden. Some others have a demonic experience and they pass out. The last thing they remember is their eyes shutting and they can't tell what followed afterward.

Understand this: such things are not supposed to happen to you; and if they've been happening to you, you can stop them by applying the power of the Holy Spirit.

In His ministry to Jesus, we read in Luke 22:43 that as an Angel from heaven, He strengthened Jesus. Now, He strengthens you. Listen to the Spirit's prayer through Paul the Apostle:

> ***"That he would grant you, according to the riches of his***

glory, to be strengthened with might by his Spirit in the inner man..."

(Ephesians 3:16).

The Spirit strengthens you with might in your inner man. Bless God, the Holy Ghost is your strengthener!

The Standby

The last operation of the Holy Spirit mentioned, which is so beautiful, is the word *Standby*: He's your Standby. When you run out of everything - your strength, information, ideas and options - there is a standby, the Holy Spirit; and He never fails. When things fail in your life, He'll show up. He's your Standby.

He's like a standby generator. When

you run out of the electricity and the power source shuts down, a standby generator kicks off immediately so you can continue to enjoy all the nice things of life.

The doctors may tell you that your heart is not pumping right or that your kidneys are not working right. They may have told you that your lungs are not functioning well and everything seems to be shutting down. I want you to know that there's a Standby.

The Bible says,

> ***"But if the Spirit of Him who raised Jesus from the dead dwells in you, He who raised Christ from the dead will also give life to** (vitalize) **your mortal bodies through His Spirit who dwells in you"***
>
> **(Romans 8:11 NKJV).**

Can you expect a miracle today? When the Holy Spirit gets a hold of your body, He will energize every fibre of your being. Everything that wasn't functioning right in your body will suddenly receive life. You will become normal, so that you can live a normal and healthy life.

The Bible says it's by the same Spirit that raised Jesus from the dead, not another one that resembles Him. It doesn't matter where the trouble came from. It may be from a spiritual attack or from something you ate. It makes no difference; it just doesn't matter. When the Holy Ghost takes over, He will give life to your body. He will energize your spirit and supply you with the necessary requirements in knowledge, wisdom and understanding.

Chapter Three

Take Advantage of the Ministry of the Holy Spirit

Your life should always be full of joy and excitement, because you've got a Helper, Comforter, Intercessor, Advocate, Counsellor, Strengthener, and Standby. How could you lose? It's impossible for you to lose with the Holy Spirit!

The trouble with a lot of God's children is that, first of all, they're not well informed of things like this. Secondly, even when they're informed, they don't know how to take advantage of what they have.

The Holy Spirit is an awesome personality; a wonderful personality. He leaves His presence everywhere and anywhere He chooses to. He also leaves His presence in places where we are well received and on people who welcome and receive us. Oh, what a blessing this is! His presence rubs off on anything that concerns us.

We haven't yet understood this, *that everything that belongs to a child of God carries the presence of the Holy Ghost.* This was the principle Peter operated in as he walked through the streets and his shadow fell upon the sick folks laid out along his path (Acts 5:15-16). They were healed because the Holy Spirit was in that shadow! When they took handkerchiefs and aprons from Paul's body, the Holy Spirit went in those hankies. That's the power of God!

"The Fourth Man In The Fire"

The Bible tells us about Shadrach, Meshach and Abednego who were threatened by the government of the day to bow down to the king's golden image or burn in the fiery furnace. Their reply was, "We won't bow because there's only one God and to Him alone we bow!"

Well, the king was very angry and he commanded his officers to make the fire seven times hotter. This, in other words, meant, "Take it to the very limit," because 'seven' is the number of completeness.

So they made it seven times hotter, the hottest fire they could possibly make. We don't read that Shadrach, Meshach and Abednego were crying. Instead, they said, "O king, our God is able to deliver us from your fiery furnace. But we want you to know that even if He doesn't, we still won't bow!" In other words, "If it is God's will for us to die in that fire, so be it. We won't bow to your golden image!"

The king ordered them to be thrown in and so urgent was his command that the soldiers who took the three young Hebrew men didn't have enough time to escape for their own lives. As they threw them into the fire, the intensity of the heat was so great that it got them and killed them.

The young men fell down in the fire, bound hands and feet. The fire was so hot, it burnt up their bands, but they got up loosed, walking free in the furnace.

Then Nebuchadnezzar said to his aides, "Do you see what I see...? How many men did we throw in the fire?"

"Three of them," they replied.

"But I see four of them" he said, "and the fourth one is like unto the Son of God."

They threw three men into the fire but the king could see four people loose, walking freely in the fire. He called them out and said to them, "Your God is God indeed!"

Nebuchadnezzar saw the Fourth Man, but you know Him. Not only does He live with you, He also lives in you. So how can you effectively take advantage of His ministry in your life? First of all, you have to function in the Kingdom.

Functioning In The Kingdom

On your own, you may be able to do a lot but when you take advantage of the ministry of the Holy Spirit in your life you'll be able to do much more.

Jesus said, "I've chosen you out of the world." He has picked us out of the world. We don't belong here even though we live here. When the Master told us we were not of this world, He meant exactly what He said. He meant you don't belong here!

We're a special race. We belong to another Kingdom; a true Kingdom and we ought to function therein. It's a spiritual Kingdom and there are spiritual activities in there that we ought to participate in consciously. We can know when we're participating in the Kingdom; we ought to know. There are many Christians who don't even know they belong there, let alone tell that they ought to function there.

You've got to know about the Kingdom to be able to function consciously in it. Every child of God should function in some spiritual activity in the Kingdom to which we belong.

When I talk about you functioning in some spiritual activity, I'm not just talking about your going to church to carry out some assignment given you by the church. I'm talking about your human spirit – your inner man (Eph. 3:16) or the hidden man of your heart (1 Peter 3:4) – functioning spiritually and carrying out spiritual tasks in that realm.

For example, there are certain prayers that you pray that produce results in the realm of the spirit, not just because they are prayers, but because of what you're saying at the time. That's the kind of spiritual activity I'm talking about – one that produces results in the realm of the spirit.

Now, your reading this book is the Spirit's effort to engage you in the realm of the spiritual Kingdom to which you belong, because the words you're reading now are not of this world. If your spirit can get a hold of these words in the realm from which they're coming to you, you will begin to function in that realm by communicating with the Holy Ghost – receiving information, instruction and direction from Him.

Soon enough, your spirit will be ministering back to God in that same realm and you would know that you're functioning spiritually. But that's just one of the several spiritual activities that your spirit ought to engage in.

Build Your Life With Your Tongue

Never be afraid to say what the Lord says about you. This is the principle of God's Kingdom. If you don't say it, it will not work even though you believe it. By believing, it becomes real in the realm of the spirit but if you're going to see it on earth, you would have to say it.

Take advantage of the Word. Do you know that you can open doors for yourself? Yes, you can, because the Holy Ghost is in you! He's the One Who tells you what is right in the Scriptures. He's your Teacher. He helps you understand the Word. The most dangerous being in the earth is the Christian who knows the Word. To him, anything is possible.

You ought to talk this way: "I refuse to accept the wrong picture. I refuse failure. I open the doors of success. I open the doors of progress." Whenever you declare what God says about you this way, people will start asking you why you're talking that way. They'll even say you're proud, but all the times you said you were average and poor, they said, "Yeah we know you. You're poor and you've got nothing." They agreed with you and things didn't change. They didn't help you when you confessed negatively, so you don't have to worry about them now. They don't count. Keep talking. They may say, "You're just talking but we can't see it," but you just keep on talking. They'll see it soon.

You're not living an ordinary life. It only becomes ordinary through your words. When you speak ordinary words, your life becomes ordinary.

Someone might say, "Well, I don't think so." Alright then, go ahead and keep speaking ordinary words and see how ordinary your life will become.

Build your life with your tongue. That's the principle from our city. As you speak, you're laying the blocks. Stand in front of a mirror and say to yourself, "I'm a success."

You may look like the biggest fool and the biggest failure but refuse to see that. Say, "I'm a success. The world is waiting for me. I know where I'm going. I wasn't born for nothing. I can't live an empty life. I came to touch this world. I'm on my way and I can only get better."

Learn to use words; your mouth will take you places. It's with your mouth that you'll open doors. God wants to speak but He wants to do it through your mouth. Look at the road you're traveling. Are you following God's Word? Are you sticking to what the Bible says about you? Stick to it, it cannot fail.

Take Advantage Of The Anointing

To be anointed means to be rubbed in such a way as to become one. The Bible says, *"But he that is joined unto the Lord is one spirit"* (1 Corinthians 6:17). When Moses stood before the Red Sea and God said to him: *"Moses, stretch your hand over the water and divide it,"* he obeyed God and stretched his hand over the water.

At that moment, he ceased to be Moses; he became a divine creation. Why? That's because when he stretched forth his hand, the hand of God was stretched forth in him. When he spoke words, they were not the words of Moses but the words of God, for his words became anointed by the Holy Ghost.

The anointing of the Holy Ghost is for you if you're born again. If you have received the Holy Ghost, that anointing of God's Spirit will come upon everything that you do. Understand what it is to be blessed of God: It means the anointing is left on everything you touch. That anointing leads and guides you.

The economy of the world was designed to fail. It was not designed to be successful or victorious. So when you observe the economy failing, don't feel sad. You're expected to go higher. How? By applying spiritual principles through the power of the Holy Ghost.

When you give your offering, send it forth by the anointing. When you sign a cheque for the kingdom of God, send it forth by the anointing.

Use what you have right now; use it for your health, your school, your family, your children, your job and your finances. It's the anointing, use it!

I'm not talking of some oil in a bottle or a piece of cloth from an evangelist or prophet or preacher. I'm talking of the real person of the Holy Ghost and His tangible presence. Glory to His Name!

Chapter Four

The Voice of the Spirit

The Holy Spirit is a Person and not a thing. Sometimes, we think that when He ministers to us, He will speak with a loud voice. We want to feel a shaking first or we want to hear a noise. But that's not the way He ministers.

"And he said, Go forth, and stand upon the mount before the LORD. And, behold, the LORD passed by, and a great and strong wind rent the mountains, and brake in pieces the rocks before the LORD; but the LORD was not in the wind: and after the wind an earthquake; but the LORD was not in the earthquake: And after the earthquake a fire; but the LORD was not in the fire: and after the fire a still small voice. And it was so, when Elijah heard it, that he wrapped his face in his mantle, and went out, and stood in the entering in of the cave. And, behold, there came a voice unto him, and said, What doest thou here, Elijah?" **(1 Kings 19:11-13).**

Elijah was on a mountain waiting for God, and where he was waiting, several awe-inspiring events that caught his attention transpired. Although it seemed these things were loud and fearsome enough to announce God's presence, He chose not to come with them. Rather, He came with a still, small voice.

God didn't show up in a way Elijah would have expected Him to. He announced His presence with a still, small voice. If He operated like that back then, you can trust that He still operates the same way today.

The Holy Spirit talks to God's children all the time but many don't respond as they really should. More frequently than not, they respond to Him with their senses. They expect that when He talks, there should be a loud noise and a violent shaking but that's not true.

The Bible says, *"...without faith it is impossible to please him: for he that cometh to God must believe that he is, and that he is a rewarder of them that diligently seek him"* (Hebrews 11:6).

It therefore means that to hear God's voice, you have to do it by faith. It takes faith to accept 'a still small voice' as the voice of God. That's the kind of voice you hear in the nighttime as you lie in your bed, saying, "Arise son, it's time to pray."

When you hear a still, small voice or a nudging in your spirit urging you to pray, that's the Holy Spirit. Or do you think it's your mind that tells you that you haven't prayed today? Why didn't your mind tell you that before you were born again?

Do you think it's your mind that tells you that you haven't studied your Bible today or that it's time to go to Church? No, it's the Holy Ghost!

You have to learn to listen to Him. He's the One Who calms your spirit when you're angry. He's the One Who tells you everything will be alright. He gives you hope. Even when you do things wrong, He's the One who helps you out. The Bible says in the book of Isaiah,

> ***"...if you leave God's paths and go astray, you will hear a voice behind you say, "No, this is the way; walk here"***
>
> **(Isaiah 30:21 TLB).**

This is the reason you can't fail. With the Holy Ghost in you, you can't help but grow in everything you do. The Bible says when you miss your way, you'll hear a voice behind you say, "Stop! This is the way, walk in it."

It's impossible to fall into error or be defeated after hearing that Voice. Instead, you just keep winning all the way because greater is He that is in you than he that is in the world!

In our fellowship with the Holy Spirit, we come into His awesome ministry, but to receive that ministry, we must also learn to minister to Him.

In Acts 13:1-2, the Bible tells us of certain prophets and teachers who ministered to the Lord. As they did, the Holy Spirit ministered back to them and it resulted in the first missionary journey of Paul and Barnabas.

If we are to receive the ministry of the

Spirit, we must also recognize that we have our ministry to the Spirit. This is the communion of the Holy Ghost and its blessing.

To contact the author write:

Pastor Chris Oyakhilome:

United Kingdom:
Christ Embassy Int'l office
363 Springfield Road
Chelmsford, Essex, CM2 6AW
Tel:+44 1245 490 234

Please include your testimony or help received from this book when you write. Your prayer requests are welcome.

South Africa:
303 Pretoria Avenue
Cnr.Harley and Hendrik Vewoerd,
Randburg, Gauteng, South Africa.
Tel:+27 72 241 7332

Nigeria:
Christ Embassy
P.O. Box 13563, Ikeja,
Lagos, Nigeria.
Tel:+234-802 332 4187-9;
+234-1-773 7611-5

or email:pastorchris@christembassy.org